THE CURSED WEDDING NIGHT

A Collection of English Poems
in the Era of Meta-Modernism

RANJAN YADAV

INDIA · SINGAPORE · MALAYSIA

ISBN 979-8-88909-895-9

Contents

Contents

Contents

Contents

Part Three

Short Poems

Contents

Part One

Long Poems

1

Gandhi: The Legend

1

When the hot blood overflowed in the Thames,
And the London bridge was falling down—
Eliot visioned nectar in awoken-eyes,
And rushed to find peace in Indian Ocean,
To get the deadly world conscious—
And to purify the hot blood of the Thames,
Enchanting the Mantras—"Shantih, Shantih, Shantih."
He found Indian Forefathers as unhidden stars of harmony,
And Panini, perhaps as the first connector of scattered letters.
Peace and Love can't stay in the house of Anarchy,
The encroachment by invaders, is the Palace of Lust,
Molesting the Earth by mining—
Invaders are going to touch the breasts of Moon and Mars.
If diversity in ideology kills fraternity, this world would
turn into a heap of dust.

2

When the black hair of Africa was falling
Into the yards of Whites—
And Africans were showing their bald heads to the world,
Gandhi resists, and adamantly he fights,
Against the invaders and racists, to balance the world.
As herbs, wounded heart-healer, he was,
A much-flexible creeper, from root to boughs.
The form, he took, can't be fixed in a book,
A social-scientist he was, invented harmless weapons,
To shun the hunged-ills, from the world.
He pointed 'Truth' as a spiritual weapon,
And 'Non-violence' as an intellectual one
He wanted the house of hatred to be collapsed in debris,
And to ride in the Chariot of Love, Peace, Fraternity and
spirituality.

3

Cats and dogs raining, with the West Storms,
Drowned the soul of Mother-India, devastating Land's
all norms.
''Half-Naked Fakir'', Said a White-hair-head—
The very Fakir, knocked the White-hair-head, on the
thorny bed.
Oh! Unruly! All the shining gowns
Do not deserve the shining towns.
When Indians were being bereft of pleasure, and feeling pain,

The "Half-Naked-Fakir" was not hidden,
Sitting at the door of Death, he was spinning the suffocating airs,
From the mantle of the Earth, to the upper layers.
He was releasing oxygen, and reducing the onrush of the West wind,
And breaking down, the overwhelming power, of Foreign-fiend;
To wash the overshadowed smokes, filled in Indian lungs,
So that, Indians might breathe well, and voice in Indian tongues.

4

The West-wind was pouring dust in eyes, exploiting the mind,
And Gandhi was wiping the dust away, giving eyes to the blind;
Gathering Indians in mass, at the Indian halt,
To oppose offenders, through the "Satyagrah of Salt."
'Civil Disobedience' was applied as an armor,
To air the lungs of youth, woman and farmer.
While stopping the wind of the West, many a times he was locked,
Under the walls, but his voice echoed outside, the West was shocked,
And whispering about the power of Gandhi, in white feather,
"His wrinkled-bones are under the walls, but he is not hither."

Now, in a peaceful grave, his flesh does rest,
But the soul still moves to protect the Land and warns the West.
He remained a secret for the white—
And for India, the treasure of freedom-fight.

5

Culture for him, was red-blood in vein,
And Civilization, as the soul in a man.
Perceiving some parasite and vulture,
He inked 'Indian Civilization and Culture',
And signaled to the folks of Indian fertility—
'Let the parasite falter away, to save our ancient heredity'.
He had deep belief in every religion,
He saw religion as the virtuous path for human.
He worshipped Almighty, and loved the Psalm,
When the sun of life was setting, he whispered, ''Hey Ram''.
In his religious vision, God is ultimate,
So, no repentance, but good deeds may expiate
Our sins, done by our sinful earth
On this holy Earth, beginning from our birth.

6

In the Palace of politics, no legend is unblamed, so his bones
Too, as supporting bourgeoisie, and playing pro and cons,
Were blamed, and for harnessing the massive force,
And establishing himself as a political course.
'Hot milk is not drunk while boiling,

Fruit is not tasted while planting the tree and toiling.'
What is Gandhi, one may know,
If one can be his summer's snow.
As a tiny seed, he tore the crust and took birth,
And for the sake of Nation, he forsook all his mirth,
The love and power, he inserted in human-hearts,
Can't be inked and pictured in my artificial arts.
His eco-efforts got the Nation shackle's free,
And he became a huge immortal 'Gandhian Tree'.

7

When the psyche falls into the cup of charms,
Love waits for none to hold the charms in arms,
Donne rebukes, ''Old pedantic and unruly Sun'',
At loving time, what have you done?
But Sriram and Bharati wait, for Gandhi's feet,
To mingle their two hearts, into a single beat.
On this Earth, millions step down, by the same ship,
But all the folks of fertility, are not to worship.
He was an open sphere of miracle,
Of love, patience, truth and, of struggle.
He was a fair mirror, with complexion dark,
Drank the drops of poison, to become a true patriarch.
His sacrifice for patriotism, can't be counted, but we can feel,
One who wants to know him, will have to spin his wheel.

8

Where large fish eats the little fishes,
Who harkens the victims and suppressed wishes?
Here justice for trodden, peeps from fissures,
Parasites catch the neck, suck the trodden to fill their pitchers;
They are engulfed in pride, lust, wrath and sloth,
So, do not care for the houseless- hungers and tattered cloth.
The human whose heart is pure like the Ganga, thinks for the whole,
The soul that connects straight to God, can not hurt another soul.
It was' Bapu', the harbinger of love and fraternity
In India with communal-justice, equality and liberty.
One may mine the pearls, or may walk on pottery,
His stream of dreams for the Nation, was no bigotry.
The deceptive give wounds, and become wound-pelters
But Gandhi lost his breath in building others' shelters.

9

Humanity of the dead, dies not with death,
But withers the body, and stops the breath,
Flowers decompose, yet the fragrance continues,
Somewhere in flora, somewhere in unseen hues.
Before death, warriors bury their fears,
The folk of fertility, later call them martyrs.
Men are mortal, but deeds are immortal and rage,
The setting of the Sun of life, in old age.

He is the floating drops in the Indian-Pacific Ocean,
And on the farming land, drops of hopeful rain,
That irrigate human crops to keep green, for long years,
For shunning dangers and fears, and wiping tears.
As I dive deeper in Gandhian sea, I wish him to be my art,
So that I may propagate his philosophy, being his part.

10

Not huge and bold like Beelzebub, but an ill name,
Held a life-snatching weapon, ended the Gandhian-frame,
Suddenly the breathing body withered, then breath stopped,
Oh! the embodiment of truth and non-violence was chopped.
Alas! The World went wonder, looking the assassinated man,
The 'Half-Naked-Fakir' went, leaving the Nation in deep pain.
From the hole of heart, blood was bleeding—
And the seeds of love and fraternity, he was seeding...
He planted fair-seeds, in land, and in the air,
That germinated firstly in India, and then everywhere.
The school of thoughts he built, will never pass away,
It will keep bestowing energy and light, like Sun's ray.
When he died, God must have sent a chariot from heaven,
To bless, and to take him to heaven, absorbing his death-pain.

2

A Train to Patna

Beginning

Come and feel, a tour in train,
Some pit in pleasure, and cry in pain,
It's cloudy sky of september's Sun,
So sympathize in pain and laugh in fun.
People of different religions and races,
Sitting in train, as unknown faces,
All are travelling for particular purpose,
And I, as an observer, observe thus.

The Bride (Section One)

There was a beautiful bride,
And her groom, sitting in pride:
Wishing the train, reaching soon,
For, the hearts were on honeymoon.
The groom was lost in bride's charm,
O hell! Soon a goon shot in her arm,
The jingling jewells and shining gown

Faded, and the new bride fell down.
To catch the goon, the groom tried,
And in pain deep, the bride cried,
And asked holding her groom's foot,
"Who was the goon? Why did he shoot?"
The scene seemed sea of grief, groom it's slave,
He was stuck speechless, as dead going to grave.
Come and believe my beat, I'm not lying,
Travellers in train, witnessed the bride dying.

The Eunuch (Section Two)

An enchanting eunuch came there,
With waving waist and face fair,
She had a bowl, and as a bell she rang,
And some folks of eunuchs, she sang.
She was singing with harsh sound,
Jingling anklets, waving skirt round,
Makeup on face as a flirting beloved, she did,
And well-wishes for all travellers, she did bid.
As a woman, she had woman-breast,
And long cloudy hair, waving as bird's crest,
Oh! Come with me and feel the pain,
She was neither a woman, nor a man...
What to say? Youths commented many more,
Someone told eunuch, and someone told whore.
Then she beat her unfertilized breast, and did faint,
Mourning within on fate, in other boggy she went.

Lady Beggar (Section Three)

Then there came a lady of old aged,
By her sons, she had been raged,
And her husband was killed with a dagger;
So she left her home and became a beggar.
A cut-kamandal in her arm she did hang,
And with her gasping voice, she sang—
"*Dede dede oye mora Rama,*
Rabba bana dega sab tora kama."
She had worn a cleft and tattered cloth,
Some gave money, some went sloth.
Then she told the tale of her youthful hue—
"At parents' home I was a morning dew,
But fate or fault is suffocating my breath,
So I'm waiting for the agent of my death."
Listening her grief, some women wept,
And who heard as fairy-tale, they slept.

The Students (Section Four)

A students' group, in meditating ways,
Holding the hanger and hoping some rays,
Rays of future, rays of business and life-bright,
Their lives were in full of dark, they wanted light.
They were hungry, and eyes sunken deep,
Their guardians grazed cows and sheep,
Their mothers worked at other's home;

Yet they dreamt to visit London and Rome.
One of them spoke with suppressed tongue—
"My pop is poor, and an infection in his lung,
An illiterate he is, yet he toils day and night,
To make me literate, and my future bright."
Dreams and passion, buried in hearts,
Can hardly be understood by physical marts...
None was ready to recognize lives' cost,
At the age of arising, the youths were lost.

Food Sellers (Section Five)

In mid way, got in, some food sellers,
Singing and telling story, as storytellers,
One of them, a bunch of key, was ringing,
And an unknown song, he was singing—
"Khale khale eee, oo babu chana,
Hum to jayenge abki Madina."
Other one had worn a Kurta red,
And a thick turban on head,
He was selling lemon tea,
What he sang, come and see—
"Jo vi piyega, aayega itnaa maaza,
Pal ver sochega ki hummmhi hai Raaza."
Most of them were helpless heads,
Struggling for their daily breads,
Physically weak, but wordy-bold,
And thus, their goods, they sold.

The Teacher (Section Six)

After two stations, we met a teacher,
Imparting human norms as a preacher—
"In shape of human, we are worst beast,
Sunken in the sea of sin, celebrating feast,
Feast of hatred, and feast of death,
Hahaha! We celebrate of snatching breath."
"Our flesh is but the debris of a room,
That is certainly fated to doom."
As a man of wit, he talked of ethics—
"People killed the pleasure of politics,
Or as a subject, politics is not so bad,
When coming in power, men go mad."
"Science is an invention, scientists are brave.
By nature, we are digging our own grave."
He talked of religion, as a utopian city,
And marriage, a sacred bond, not a pity.

Killing of Cuckoo (Section Seven)

For a while, I peeped the outer sight,
And saw a cuckoo in trap of a kite,
Fluttering wings, struggling for liberty;
Stopped breathing in brute's captivity.
To get rid of brute, the innocence did fight...
But the brute sucked blood to quench appetite:
Other birds feared, witnessed the plight,
And bathing in blood, happy was the Kite.

The train was full of human herds,
For a while, I got human-nature in those birds,
The men of strength, keep climbing on pick,
Suppressing and sucking blood from the sick.
Laboring-lives are unable to fight for their right,
They are cut by the throat for feast, by parasite.
Here flowers too, are frightened, all the days,
For suckers suck, and harm, in different ways.

Conclusion

I was not travelling as a happy tour, but in strife,
With some pricking problem, I was going with my wife,
I marked each eye, face, luggage and gown,
Frustration existed on faces, hearts in pain, eyes down.
Who does not want a crown on his or her head,
But life is trapped in calamity, lying on a thorny bed.
I wanted to observe more traits, pain and passion,
But half-heartedly, I reached, to my destination...

3

The Death of a Childless Mother

1

She was a beauty, soul and sense was fair,
Eye-catching waxen waist, and long hair;
Her lips, parted in smile, and teeth cucumber seeds
Purged in purity, that beauty, alone God bids.
She had something-sweet, far-fetched voice,
Whoever heard that once, desired twice—
She was loved by all, kind was her heart,
None can find this veiled-beauty at any mart.

2

Beauty of bride sparkled under the new veil,
She was pregnant of goodness, like Sita's tale,
At marriage time in *Mandap*, when she did sit,
She felt her inside, dancing of her heart-beat;
And rhythmic tempo of some singing sound,
Like, "By fate, a good groom, I have found."
She sat on the top of the happiest tower,
And travelled from bud to blossomed-flower.

3

She shifted in new shelter, at in-law's home,
Leaving her Birth-Earth, dear dad, and mom,
And sprinkled the fragrance of youthful hue,
Dropping on her groom, as morning dew.
Surya, her groom, was a famed-farmer,
And guarded his family as an iron-armor.
Soon they saw, the rising Sun in the east,
They became parents, and gave a feast.

4

The new born-baby, Champa, lived few days,
Soon doomed-day came, the rising Sun lost rays,
Alas! The pleasure of being a mother had gone...
She scolded God, "O God! What have you done?"
Oh! The Hope of home, now, you are dead,
And neighbours are preparing your death-bed.
Unstopping tears sprang, from each and every eye,
Brooding over the pearl, oh! How did she die?

5

Sometime before, a mother, she had been,
And was honoured, as a fortunate queen;
But now, the child wrapped in coffin, went,
And as a childless mother, her head was bent.
She became an empty-woman, heart-broken,
The heartbeat once danced, drowned in pain...

She cried and in gasping voice did murmur,
"O God! The love I lost, how can I conquer?"

6

Champa seemed very promising and brave,
An emblem of Lakshmi, embraced the grave.
The pleasure of the mother turned into a frost,
Yet, she collected courage and smiled as a ghost.
After losing Champa, a pearl, that had gone,
She gathered hope to be conceived with other one.
Counting as days and months, passed years,
She could not conceive, so she shed tears.

7

Once, while passing through the way, she heard
The taunt, *'Banjh'* (childless), that women whispered.
Laughing life was trapped in the whirling gyre,
And internally, she began to burn without fire.
She lost her child, majesty, and everything,
Became a corpse in shape of woman-being;
For, her husband humiliated her too,
Now, a lone lady, what will she do?

8

One day with makeup, she wore a *saree* red,
'Oh! Mom and dad have died', the lady said,
'O God! Now no way to walk, where to go,
When a groom deceived a wife, whom to bow?'

In stereotyping culture, she lost her might,
And the broken-bride, could not fight.
Then Surya married to an other wife,
For deteriorating more, her love-lost life.

9

How our socio-mental structure is built,
Why Surya changed? What was her guilt?
Without a child, has a woman no worth?
Assuming so, is a dangerous ditch on Earth.
This *sautan* (other wife) was a lady of mean-mood,
Who deprived the childless mother, from food,
And used to abuse, like "damn, doomed and whore,
Get lost *Banjh,* what will you do living more"?

10

She too was a mother, but now no more,
Now neighbours too abuse, as calling whore.
The spirit of her sprouting life had gone,
Leaving a heap of flesh in her weaker-bone.
She lost her queen-majesty with daughter's death,
Oh! Now as a doomed-mother, takes empty breath,
And bears broken-fate, on the thorns, she leans,
And mourns the fate, O God, I did, what the sins!

11

Her sphere had shrunk, breath filled with obstacles,
No man's mercy, life is fettered in fate's shackles,

The death angel took away her dear dad and mom,
Husband deceived, Champa died, now no hope, no home...
In pain deep, she went severely sick, no one to care,
So she left her home for a forest to find a shelter there,
But couldn't bear the remembrance of daughter's death,
So, wrapped a rope in her throat, and stopped her breath.

4

A Little Illusion of India

1

In Hell or Heaven, none takes birth,
Every human has a lease of the Earth
Gifted by God, pouring the same blood,
But the water of illusion, flows as flood.
Sometime, I look the affect of hatred,
That makes the people separate,
With castes, religions, as Islamism or Hinduism,
Where all hold one religion, that is humanism.

2

I wonder, in colour, what can be seen?
Hindus prefer red, and Muslims, green,
What the flowers bid! Burn in hating-heat,
Marigolds in temples, Lilies in Mosques fit.
Face fair and heart dark, is the door of hell,
In ill-trap, all children of Mother-India fail
In blossoming India's beauty and purity...
Let's gather all the broken hearts, in one bowl of unity.

3

To unite the world, the world demands sacrifice,
But some souls seem freezing, as freezing of ice,
Sacrifice! Not of buffaloes, goats or any other cattle,
Sacrifice of jealousy, hatred and all, that are fatal.
Pain of death seems less, when one hates another man,
Making him alien, thinking so much unusual pain,
And imagines at hot-noon, as if others were not there,
Majesty would kiss the feet, the world would be so dear.

4

Thorns of illusion prick the soul, how it can be seen,
By Her, whose children, lost in dark, are getting ruin.
India is Sita's mother, she is beyond stronger,
But can't bear the conflicts of children, as a Mother.
She teaches all novices," all shall die who are born,
Learn from a flower, who learns to live with a thorn.
Lie dies with birth, all those are truth, those exist,
Love and peace are heritage of human, not of beast."

5

Genders look like the fissure of rocks,
Women, below as sparrows, men sitting as hawks:
With the birth of a daughter, fates confine,
With the birth of a son, the same fates shine.
Let's fill the fissure of genders with equality,
Let women get equal chance, instead of getting pity;

They are the roots and stems of human creation,
Mothers of all kings, truth, love, peace and passion.

6

Wipe my tears with perfection, when I think deep,
I weep, and sometimes in night,I have no sleep,
Who sowed the seeds, by which men are discriminated,
As if castes and religions are written on the head.
Who imposed so many castes, who became caretakers,
As Milkmen, Oilmen, Goldsmith, butcher or Shoemakers?
Hence I appeal, let's blossom love, mingling all creeds,
Cutting the tree of discrimination, burning all its seeds.

7

Slavery is the son of brutes, but following religion's purity,
Is as Father, to his children, hands duty;
And assisting in each other's duty is worth,
That brings among all, love, peace and mirth.
In India, Akbar established Ilahi Religion,
Before, Elizabeth in England did bid Anglican;
Anyway, their golden efforts were same
To unite different religions, giving one name.

8

Kings do efforts for betterment, but courtiers deceive,
They eat the meat, bit by bit. And bones, they leave.
From Nehru to now, criticizers deserve to blame,
But all of them worked for India's glory and fame.

Observing illusions, Kings make laws, when in rein
But while planting, who pours sweetness in sugarcane?
Government is a tree, its bodies are short and length,
Branches of selfishness must be cut, for country's strength.

9

India, our Land, is great in Asia,
Even greater than Italy and Russia,
For, She has a mild democracy—
Where, they have smell of past aristocracy.
When this little illusion of caste and religion,
From this great land, will be gone,
The message of love and peace from here,
Will walk faster than the rays of sun, to everywhere.

10

She is the heart of Asia, Her people, pearls of undug mine,
Sitting in ecstacy, on the throne of diversity, she does shine,
And sprinkles her bright light, on her all children,
To show them the path of spirituality, and absorbs their pain.
We children are scattered flowers, Mother makes us garland;
Whenever this garland breaks, Her children must mend.
As she is huge, we need working hard, depending less on fate,
To make Mother more mighty, to make Mother more great.

5

Come Conscious

Where is Liberty?
If the trodden people are suffering,
At the hands of exploiters or suffocators;
If the tongues of troddens are pressed within,
Scolding as, ''Hold your tongues, you are mean—''
Where is justice?
If the criminals from the house of kings, fly,
And commoners are caged...
Where is peace?
If the name of religion,
is more safe than human—
And the human sow the seeds of hatred,
And burn in the flame of jealousy—
Where is equality?
If children of kings go to study America and Spain,
And the sons of sweepers sweep the drain—
If the farmers, labours and Nation builders sleep in open sky,
And the people who consume them, sleep in the Palace high—
Where is happiness?

If the promising youths are wandering
Unemployed, losing their hopes—
And hope-broken parents,
Shed tears hiding in the corner of the house—
Where is love?
If lovers are lynched with the arrows of,
Caste, religion and family-dignity—
If in old age, we leave our parents, who give us lives,
On the complaining of neighbours and wives—
Where is brotherhood?
If we fight on the fort of diversity.
Without thinking far,
Some countries begin war,
The desire of Nation's expansion is lust,
That may turn the world into dust.
O the world! Where are you, and where am I?
Have we taken birth, to eat, to fight and then to die?
Or to change the dehumanizing things—
And to sow the seeds of fair human beings...

6

The Cursed Wedding Night or
The Wife of a Soldier

Section One: Blossoming

1

When water from the high-hills, falls in drops,
Millions of peasant be optimistic to water the crops:
For feeding foods to all the hungers—
To make them artists, singers and mighty soldiers.
Here is born a baby girl, and growing as creepers,
She grew young, and beauty held as Helen...
And for soothing her heart, she began to quest a man.

2

A Soldier was on his holiday, climbing on a hill,
There Helen's beauty dazzled his eyes, heart began to feel;
A strong stream of love, so, he tried to woo her, to marry,
To add the taste in fleeing life, as in betel, red-red cherry;
Helen too was in quest, soon the soldier's love was granted.

They got their parents in confidence, and took seven round,
Here, the soldier's wife tells her story, in her own sound.

3

I had a divine garden, with full of trees and fruits,
I kept hiding the fruits from the wild beast,
And wanted my groom to have, as a Love-feast.
My desire met to destination, the heavenly hour came:
With shyness, I parted my lips, whispered God's name.
O God! Trees of my garden would change into woods,
Today, I would serve my groom, the spiritual Love-foods.

4

In happiness heart was humming, it was first night,
Chamber was decorated with dappled light,
Multicoloured flowers were dispersed on the bed,
And I, as a bride in dazzling gown, as cherry-red
Was feeling sweet sensation of unfolding my charms,
And wanted to unveil my veil, to hide in my husband's arms.
I wanted to bathe in the tub of love, with his gentle touch.

5

I was sitting on my bed, with triangle-eye, and a bit-bent-head,
I felt of being on heavenly tour, when he knocked the door,
I was lost in happiness, but heartbeat hastened, unlike before.
He entered inn, below the bed he stood, and for a long he gazed,

And gifted a gold-ring for showing face, then my veil, he
raised..
And whispered, "O the beauty, where you had been,
No fairies match, If I compare, I'll commit unforgiven sin."

6

Then he held my hand with his gentle touch, and said,"
"O the beauty! I thank the God, by whom you are made,
I wish this night to be longer than a decade,
So that your mortal blossomed beauty may not fade!"
Then I held his hand coming closer, and whispered,
"You too are so handsome, o my swooning dove,
Since night is short, let's play the game of love."

7

No sooner did the beauty of the bride was unveiled
Than the heavenly hour changed into hell
With the ringing of the telephone's damned bell.
Alas! On the dappled bed of Love, he left
My burning beauty with unseen fire,
And for the sake of nation's rest,
He prioritized his duty, being a lady's lier.

8

In no time, he changed, from a groom to a soldier,
And at the eleventh hour, on my head, he kissed,
Holding my hand in his hand, he promised
Of returning soon, and said only this,

''Sorry dear Devi, I'll have to go for nation's peace,
Ah! With the bottom of my heart, I'll miss.''
I could not utter any word, my voice was' hiss'.

9

I became dumb, my eyes were full of tears,
All the sense of love was bridged with fears.
Blood of patriotism runs in his veins, for nation's sake,
O God! My man is going to fight on death-stake...
Bless him with undefeated power, keeping me hopeful!
I too will defeat the fate, as a soldier's wife,
And I will wait for my man, to my whole life.

Section Two: Fading

10

Since my man went, the hour of setting sun,
Seemed to me like a long dungeon...
I did not get slumber, the whole night,
Remembering my man, I turned side by side;
The dappled beauty on bed, as a green grass in desert.
The bedsheet with the picture of love and divine wine,
Was saddened and wetted with the tears of mine.

11

Deploying at border, my man wrote a letter, titled 'Dear',
Inside the letter, '' There is no holiday for a year."
In a dream at night, I saw the death of desire,
And without rain and thunder, blowing off the fire.
I cut my fingers with my teeth, with messing words—
''Ram Re Ram", What the hell brought the turmoil!
Beauty burns in bed, and the groom went to save the soil.

12

Then I consoled my hollow-heart...
To beat the tattered time, and not to flirt,
There was fire in my heart, but I suppressed the flame,
Taking the oath of my husband's name.
Yet, sometimes, I wished to move,
In other's garden to test the fruits of love,
For quenching my hunger and thirst.

13

Desire is a deep-dug ditch, nothing can suffice,
To save the turban of a soldier, let me sacrifice.
I'll save the turban of my father and father-in-law,
I'll preserve the prestige of my mother and mother-in-law.
I'll grow in God's grace, let me play in the womb of dignity
And protect the honour and glory of all relation,
Let me shed my tears, suppressing my emotion.

14

Now the span of the year was to move in round,
And my deserted garden, was to turn in a green ground,
It was in want of thunder, lightening and heavy rain
For the petal suffered a long drought with pricking-pain.
One Sun hid in clouds, the clouds brought the rain of love,
And I found my man stepping to me, as a swooning dove.
When love comes to meet, none can stop one's hurrying feet.

15

Long drought sufficed, but I knew the Second-Moon's light,
It comes to provoke dreamers, then there must be dark night.
Pleasures overwhelmed and eyes filled with tears,
Tears of happiness, but suddenly heart felt fears,
Fears of fifteen years, yet he assumed me not to worry,
Whenever there is a holiday, he will hurry.
In a year, he came once or twice to provoke my senses.

16

Once he came on a long leave, and I was conceived,
I wanted my man to stay more, but the fate deceived…
Alas! Again he went, conceiving a child in my womb
As the corpse bearers leave the corpse in a tomb.
I cared the womb-baby as a queen, and gave birth,
I cried, 'O my man I will die, hellish is the labor-pain!'
None helped,there was not my man, I cried in vain.

17

The house of my comfort was in my convulsion,
The particles of my heart scattered, without eruption.
Now that time has gone, my heart has found other desire,
The desire of motherly-love, with fading flame of youthful
fire.
The garden that suffered drought, has planted a tree of
pleasure.
Now my happy playing child is my love, comfort and
treasure;
It's laughing lips burn the candle of comfort, in my heart.

18

Now fifteen years has passed, having retired he has come,
Now I, a mother of three children, live in a mother-dom.
One morning I saw a blossomed flower, it seemed bride's
bed,

Alas! with the setting of the Sun, it did fade,
The hue and fragrance that fascinated the visitors, went,
And for the hovering bees, it has no taste, no scent.
O the gardener! when the flower fades, it seems dead.

7

My Mother: An Iron Lady

Father died, I was only five or six month old,
I can't remember his face, my mother said,
Not a rich man he was, but a common villager,
With some piece of land and two oxen to farm.
Mother said, 'Production of crops was not enough
To maintain the family for the whole year—
So he used to go to Kolkata to earn money.

Happiness doesn't seek a house of richness or poverty,
It's a psychological asset, no mart to buy and sell,
A hermit can be more happy than a crowned king.
My mother said,"We were happy with what we had,
But when fortune falls, God becomes helpless—
This time he sowed crops and went to Kolkata to earn,
Alas! He did never come back, even dead body did not
return.

My mother lived in Asnatari, a village in Banka district,
Bihar,
When she heard, the earth under her feet, went down,

She wanted to go to see the corpse of my father,
Oh! There was none to take her to kolkata—
A wife could not meet to her husband, even at the last moment...
Her heart was torn as glass falling on floor—
My cousin brothers who worked there, burnt his dead body.

The untimely death of dad, shocked my mother,
As if a callous cloud, full of calamity had fallen down.
Bringing up five children, was crossing the sea without ship,
But we five siblings were her bridge of hopes and dare,
Rays of strength, happiness and the reason of living.
She gathered days and nights in a single lamp as the fuel for light,

She worked at home, she worked in farming-field as a man...

My maternal grand mother gave a buffalo to my mother,
She grazed, she fed fodders, she milked herself—
And went five kilometers far on feet to sell milk,
What the heavy rain, what the melting summer...
In bitter-winter dawn, she crossed a small river,
Her heel, sole and legs shivered in bitter cold water,,
When she returned home, she basked, lighting wooden-fire.

She is a pure village lady wrapped in the shawl of maternity,
She did never bow down her honour, she held her head high,
She is a lady of dare and inspiration, she always talked fair—
As time passed, she tore the dense cloud of calamity,
And centered her scattered concentration on her children
Forgetting the pricking-pain of the death of her soul-mate.
Looking her dare and strength, the villagers called her 'an
iron lady'.

8

Dogs in a Democratic Land

In a Democratic land,
Dogs hailed the supremacy;
When feast came to feet,
One dog barked and bit another,
To be chaired as the realm's father.
When one dog was beaten and wounded,
In no time, so-called supremes
Sacrificed their slumber;
And the Democratic Court awoke at midnight,
To count the number and to resolve the fight.

Food-givers of dogs were Cats and Rats,
Who were coaxed to get safety and shelters,
From the faithful dogs, being awoken...
When the Cats ate the Rats,
When the Rats threatened the Cats,
When the Cats raped the Rats...
When the Rats tumbled here and there,
In hearts, having full of fear:
The Democratic Court slept at mid-day,

Coaxing the Cats and Rats to find some way.
In getting justice for the weak bones, it took years,
Till then the victims died in harness and fears.

The dilemma of Cats and Rats was,
Providing foods to deceptive Dogs,
And assuming the Dogs, faithful...
Kept the deceptive Dogs far from blame.
When the so-called wise, the Cats and the Rats,
Would come in conscious, dilemma would be no more.
Then there would be the Court for lives,
Not particularly for the leading animals,
There would be the Court for individuals.
O the so-called wise beings, come in light,
Perceive the Dogs' ways, and fight for your right,
Don't hide in a cave, death is worthier than being a slave.

9

Time to Change

Gift of God, one gets once, is Life,
Make the majesty like a queen, not as wife.
The drops of blood in your vein,
Are equal red, and runs as fast as in men.

Then let the patriarchal laws be broken—
No woman will be a domestic hen,
Suffocating breath in cages, with tumbling legs,
For quenching men's hunger, and filling their bags.

If, after the marriage, a woman can
Leave her father's home, then why not a man?
Has God written on some sphere or land,
That woman must live at the home of husband?

If so, then disobey the unruly God,
And sweep the laws away, with your mighty rod;
And on the same land, write with your own pen,
"No woman will leave her father's home, but a man."

Or compel the laws, for equal justice,
Where a woman may live, where she does wish,
Or a husband will live at wife's home
And the wife will be the queen of the queen-dom.

Some brutes in shape of men, hunt and eat,
The flesh of flesh, bit by bit—
And leave the lives fleshless bones...
What the drums? And what the tones?

10

Talk Between Alive and Dead Leaves

In the parching sun of summer,
I halted beneath a Banyan tree,
And in the breeze of the west wind,
On the tree, and down the tree,
The Leaves were talking—

Some were green, some were red,
Some of them were dried-and-dead...
I looked, and my sense had sunk
In the shaking branches and still trunk;
The Leaves were talking—

The green were asking to Red-and-Dead,
Why are you motionless under our shade?
Parting away from different branches,
Some weep in the woods, some in tranches...
The Leaves were talking—

You can not absorb the Sun's ray,
Neither do you know, night and day,
And wander lifelessly, hither and thither
Like a bird's fallen-feather...
The Leaves were talking—

A leaf replied, from the wailing woods,
On the behalf of Red-and-Deadhoods—
'We too, were adhered to branches one day,
And like you, we absorbed the Sun's ray...'
The Leaves were talking—

We were also as green as you are,
And bestowed breath, near and far,
Birds and herds rested in our shade,
But we lost our greenness, now we are dead...
The Leaves were talking—

11

Welcome Song for Freshers

O the rays of knowledge, and treasure of wisdom!
We lay the palms, before your feet,for your welcome,
Welcome! Welcome! Today each and every heart feels,
The fragrance of freshers, from forest, rivers and hills:
Inhaling your fragrance, watching your stepping feet,
Our palpitations in happiness, have started to beat;
Our hearts are happy, for welcoming each new face,
Into the world of knowledge and sages, through this holy
place.

Flowers are lying in way, dappled, white and crimson-red,
The Sun is peeping from cloud, as dim light, on a bride's bed
The Moon is smiling under her seven-folded veil,
Eclipsed by the Sun light, with her pressed lips, she does tell
Welcome Freshers! Welcome! Though I am not near,
Yet I feel your fragrance, meet your hearts, and make my
dear.
The waves of sea are singing, 'O the wisdom! O the wisdom,
Welcome! Welcome! in the world of wits, welcome,
welcome'!

Reptiles are dancing on surface, sparrows singing in the sky,
Wheat plants are whistling, and fairies on the mountain high.
Enthusiastically, sitting on hive, the honey bees are humming,
Welcome! All are laying their palms for your warm welcoming.
In the womb of future, who can predict, pleasures and pains,
When this fragile-frame vanishes, the remembrance remains;
Then, for the moment, let us forget all our material goals—
For making acquaintance of one soul with other souls.

Today all the breathing-beings are singing, 'O the Freshers'!
Welcome! Welcome! In the world of wits, welcome, welcome.

12

Who Care For Nature?

1

Do not drop your tears,
Your mother isn't sick, and dad has not died—
Some mining-mountains have collapsed down,
So, the roots of some rivers have dried.
Oo! People living on the banks of the rivers,
Are crying of hunger and thirst—
Go and console them, the king will water their crops.
The Earth is full of human fairs, but for Nature, who cares?

2

The Ganga who is worshipped as the Mother-Holiest,
And supposed the sinners getting expiation after a bath,
Is suffering herself from the suffocation of breath—
She is mother of many lives, living in her womb,
And hope of uncounted peasants residing on her bank,
For making their singed crops green...

Now this holy Ganga washes the filths of wealthy towns,
Garbages from industries are dusting, Mother Ganga's
gowns.

3

Unfathomed pure water runs in her vein,
And quenches the thirst of millions of lives,
But we the people cut her heart, assuming a dustbin...
And inject poison in her vein, committing a great sin.
People burn their dead kinships on her bank,
And immerse the remains of corpses in her heart—
What a superstition! Mother Ganga does not eat,
The flesh of that unburnt corpses, even a bit.

4

poisonous waste materials from industries,
Through drain and heavy rain, in rivers, sink—
O Coleridge! '' Water, water everywhere, but no drop to
drink"
When standing in a huge body of water we die of thirst,
We shall remember the sacrifice of your Albatross.
We need water to digest our feast, without it what can exist?
In the parching sun of summer, in the forest, on the
mountain high,
Animals and birds quest here and there, and thirsty they die.

5

Human being is as worthy as an insect,
In Nature's view, this is the fact.
We want fresh air passing in our lungs,
But the forest, ' The Lungs of the Planet' is burning,
Oxygen providing green trees are turning into ashes;
Thousands of lives are losing their lungs—
The roaring of tigers in the heart of forest, is turning into silence:
And flying birds with burning wings are falling down...

6

Human is worthy, but Nature doesn't lie only in human herds,
What's about trees, hills, rivers, oceans, animals and birds?
We build safety and shelters for our children and wives,
In tempest, in thunder, who cares the unsheltered lives?
When hurricane comes, the human hide in bunker or cave,
Neighbour birds and wild lives cry in pain, none goes to save.
We want the strength of our bones, and belly thick,
Molesting the prestige of Nature, and making her sick.

7

Look the lovely lizard, walking on wall—
And the peaceful tiny ant, in no agony,

The worm under the earth, is no harm,
It strengthens the soil in the field of farm.
With colourful little wings, butterflies fly,
And playing children wave hands, saying bye, bye.
The spider builds its home releasing its own filament,
When Night sleeps in the arms of darkness, Owls be vigilant.

8

Look the green grass, from inside of the Earth,
It sprouts into petal, and twinkles in greenness,
And then suffices the hunger, bestowing mirth—
To sheep, goats, cows and all grazing cattle.
Everything on the Earth, or the tiniest birth,
When comes in Nature's spinning, it has meaning.
The green grass too serves, and deserves as a being...
It sacrifices its greenness for the sake of hungry cattle.

9

Here is a Tree, my neighbour,
A tree quiet and calm—
Expanded branches, round and round,
Bestows the shelter to birds and bees,
With no rent—
Roots rooted deep, trunks ascending to sky,
Monkeys leap and nightingales sing, sitting on high.
Some climbed creepers, wrapped in branches are hung,
And leaves in ecstacy, communicate in leafy-tongue.

Leaves release greenness and refined breath,
Sustaining serenity to the environment.

The romance of spring with trees,
Results into mouth-watering fruits—
Changing the taste of tongue;
Shrunk by the freezing winter.

Goodness coheres from root to bough,
Portraying in poetic art, it seems tough—
Boughs resemble to human bodies,
Oh! The doings of bodies, get crown
And the boughs of tree are cut down—
The tree goes dumb, bearing the carnage,
Shedding tears and looking at its slaughter.

Part Two

Sonnets

1

The Poet's Prayer

O the power unseen—
Human is, but a sign of sin,
And I too, sometime, do,
And then before you, I woo,
To beg the healing-herbs,
that parching pain absorbs.
This decaying flesh is no treasure,
But a bowl of pain and pleasure.

Who weighs! How mighty you be!
None can harken, none can see
your religious ray, your walking way,
None can say, none can say.
But the soul urges you, to shun
The sin that this flesh has done.

2

Ode to Women (One)

You are the source of procreation, yet for men not suffice,
From your womb men come, yet you are preys of prejudice,
Men weighed your physical-frailty, in the machine of mind;
You have might-unfathomed, but by men, your fates were signed.
Every king or warrior comes from your womb,
Your born-babies are buried in every tomb.
You are the greatest sacrificer, as you, who can sacrifice?
O the Goddess of procreation! Yet for men not suffice.

I wander library after library, each seems the same...
In history, in journals, I quest your prestige and name,
Identities are lost in tangles, mere place in history or literature,
You were called mother, but got prestige as a domestic creature.
Men saw summer as the month of june and they did swoon,
When the beauty of flesh faded, you were a tasteless monsoon.

3

Ode to Women (Two)

You are an embodiment of power, I read in tale,
Walk on burning path and throw the imposed veil,
You are Earth, without you, no seeds, no root,
Child was emancipated who washed your foot.
Human world is a desert, and woman a green grass;
Womb, the humanely-heaven, no world can surpass.
Power can't be counted weighting physical bones,
Thy power can break the rocks-row into small stones.

This world is but a wound of flattery and disguise,
Thou, queen of kindness, in each vein true love lies,
Imagination of humanity, without you is skyian-far,
Mother of procreation! You can make, you can mar.
Measureless power! None can beat you, none can tease
You can fight, as Maa Durga to preserve your prestige.

4

Ode to Wife (One)

This is a quite true-tale, in a wife's concerning,
This world has witnessed a wife, alive burning,
In custom of '*Sati Pratha*', on husband's pyre,
The man bound in custom, was more cruel than fire.
If she was a new bride wearing bangles and *Saree* red,
No matter, she had to burn alive, if husband was dead,
With that cruel custom, a bride's dream and desire,
All were burnt in flame, by cruel men in innocent fire.

People looked burning parts as fair of mart,
Who peeped into the bride's weeping heart,
Even a spark of fire, none can bear on skin,
What sin can be more heinous than this sin?
Look the custom, only a wife suffered the pain,
If a wife was dead, the husband could marry again.

5

Ode to Wife (Two)

In the Ramayana who can forget Sita's ordeal,
She beat the drums of innocence, and did appeal,
Painful cry brought tempest all around,
What was crime? No crime this world found,
As an embodiment of truth, she did bow,
O Lord Rama! Why did you do so?
From the Lord's Palace, Goddess was banished,
In the lap of Mother-Earth, in ordeal she vanished.

In God's era or human reign,
A wife suffered unmeasured pain,
O God! Thou held the universe in thy ring,
To weaken the flying-force of wife's wing,
You may be the embodiment of truth and peace,
Under the lap of Earth Sita hid, but got no justice.

6

Ode to Wife (Three)

Wife is a huge tower of tolerance,
For house a soft flowery-fence
That absorbs the internal tussles,
And stops the strife that outside bustles.
Beauty lies in the eyes of beholders,
Not in sprouting breast, not in slim shoulders,
Not in black-blue eyes, not in catchy waist,
Not in hurting heart,not in jokes and jest.

In time-tense, she keeps humble voice,
No desire, no demand and no choice,
Without telling anything, everything, she gets,
Hovering the shadows of Saturn and ill-fates.
In harmony, time doesn't count in day or night,
Wife is a sign alive, all the time, burning love's light.

7

Ode to Wife (Four)

The world is a temple, and people as pilgrimage,
Some are maligned minds, some as sacred sage,
O man! Where thou quest temple, its within you,
You will get wages in life-wallet of what you do.
Only way of prolonging life, how can she be weak?
Shame! On wife's name, society's psyche is sick.
All sick? No, not at all, all are not sick-born,
Wife is a flower, has no enmity, even with thorn.

A house without a wife, what does exist?
Night is pregnant with dark, day with mist,
In a king's Palace, big walls have no worth,
Love-room weeps in loneliness, sofa has no mirth.
O the maligned minds, being mental-blind,
Here is Goddess, where do you wander to find?

8

Ode to Wife (Five)

It befell once, I walked in worse,
In arising-island, I felt a curse.
My neighbours came and went,
They laughed instead of lament,
I had lost all my might and mirth,
I had no hope to step on the earth.
As an angel of boon, came my wife,
She fought with fates, to save my life.

Striking my scattered hair, she ensured,
O love! Have hope, you will be cured,
I gazed and held her hand, and then left,
Covering my face with a handkerchief, I wept.
For my welfare, she toiled a lot, I did feel,
I was cured, and crossed that high hill.

9

The Burning Ghat (One)

In body-burning Ghat, crying crowd,
Some with sound gasping, some loud,
Some carrying the corpse on shoulders,
Some looking like meek beholders.
The flame of fire, from pyre, sparked;
On the bank of the Ganga, I marked.
Holding the hurt-heart in pain deep,
I saw, setting on fire of own kinship.

Here the king loses his crown,
And the pride of people falls down,
Death doesn't differ in town or village,
In caste, in religion, in illiterate or sage;
Death is inevitable, it is Nature's game,
At the time of death, all are the same.

10

The Burning Ghat (Two)

It was my mother-in-law, I was in pain,
Wet slipping-soil in way and heavy rain,
Fearful lightning and thunder was there,
Yet we went to Ghat and we saw there fair,
Fair of corpses and their crying kinships,
Fair of droplets of tears, and shivering lips,
People were setting the pegs of pyre,
And the *Dom Raja* was preparing fire.

Suddenly I cried while putting a piece of wood,
Oh! She bestowed love, money and delicious food!
She was pretty, a well natured woman,
She was an emblem of love and human,
Till the last breathing, she did toil,
But she was soil, so vanished into the soil.

11

The Burning Ghat (Three)

I gazed the burning of body, part by part,
O God! Where lies mind, soul, and heart!
Where lies love, hatred, and jealousy,
Where lies faith and the fort of fallacy,
Where lies family and farming field,
Where lies the honour and it's shield,
O God! Where lies? Where lies—
Where lies that everything, when one dies...

Life and death is Your law and art,
Here, human being is a mere part,
As a plant comes with stems and leaves,
Human comes with all those believes.
every being is on lease, soul is a worth,
It comes from Earth, it goes in Earth.

12

The Burning Ghat (Four)

With an odorous corpse, a son came,
None of us asked his native or name,
''O mother! Hey mother!'' He did mourn,
Putting his hand on head as a horn—
''How lovely and worthy you had been!
But today I have brought you in a coffin!
In less age, you died, it is extreme pain,
May God give you place in heaven!''

He seemed poor, less wood, he had brought,
In pocket, no money, so with *Dom*, he fought,
It was frightened and heart-rending scene,
He left the corpse unburnt in the coffin—
The day was rainy, he went far away,
May the Sun bless her with His sacred ray.

13

Lifelogy

On the crust, I was a human seed,
No might, no mirth and no meed,
What I had, was quick appetite;
And the time, as day and night:
Father! No! No! He was dead,
And when I felt that, my mother fed.
Little body, and mind was a petal,
Prone to blossom, without a battle.

When I grew up, I was no seeds,
I felt hung in neck, a knot of needs,
My saddened fate falters in dark;
Yet, as a rootless tree, I embark,
My hope won't stop, in sun or shade,
I will escort my life to my deathbed.

14

Friendship

Let this friendship bestow on us new wings to fly,
High, and touch the sky,
Along with wandering clouds far and far,
Under the veil of solacing moon and twinkling star;
Leaving the gender miles away,
Forgetting the term of time, night and day,
Let this grow like rainy weeds—
Let this spread all over like airy seeds.

Let this tiny seed of friendship be a woods;
That would bestow shelter and leafy foods,
To those who are ticked to depart,
From friends, lovers and kinship, breaking heart.
May it be a boon for making the spirit celestial,
Creating the cosmos of love, where all our fantasies get real.

(R & S)

15

Transition of Soul

Let me throw the black gown,
And kiss white-brown—
I want bewilderedly, to kiss,
Till there is water for fish.
I feel You, each and every moment,
By that soul and sense, I got on rent.
By body I am yours:
Without you I have no force.

Then my whole psyche wants to kiss,
God! For nothing, but for gentle bliss.
Black within body, is a smell of plight,
My soul wants to change it into white,
Not torturing this physical meet,
God! Submitting and kissing thy feet.

16

The Beauty of Setting Sun

Raptures from diversity, what these mean!
Suddenly, I was mingled in
Nature's tantalizing tease,
Forgetting my fleshy lease.
How the glory of the Sun!
Gives, the whole universe, energetic fun,
In diversity, when going down,
Looks red, yellow, bright and brown.

The chirping-birds and humming bees,
On the Earth, glorious-green trees,
over the tree, under the sky, a flying lark,
Farmers leaving the field, and lovers park.
When the shining Sun was to be sunk,
It thrilled me into, like a little drunk.

17

The Beauty of Rising Sun

With the crimson red, lifts the veil of night,
And, for all the lives, brings new light,
The tiger comes out from the cave;
The ghost vanishes into the grave.
Birds from trees, women from bed,
Awake from an unconscious shade.
Peasants feed their ploughing cattle,
For fighting nation's starved-battle.

Men of coats remain slept in coats,
And shipmen sail their empty boats.
The fish of the Ganga go down,
Looking at the Sun in His crown.
Lost in oblivion, men's mind might be absent,
But everyday, with red ray, the Sun is present.

18

The Womb-Child

Womb-child in the creepers of maternity,
Knows not the world, nor the eternity.
Womb alike tomb, but not of death,
Here is breath through mother's breath.
In the dark room, no sense of day or night,
Fights till nine months, to see the light.
Falling of drops in dark, human begins here,
Till, the tiny breaths in the womb, has no fear.

Womb-child in the creepers of maternity,
knows not the world of sins and purity,
Quite in peace, beyond the world of turmoil,
Wrapped in the layers of the filament as a coil;
As a sinner, waits long for heavenly rain,
But does not get that fate, till the labour pain.

19

School and Teacher

A confluence of two streams,
Here fills the optimistic dreams,
Shunning the darkness, fetching light,
Consciousness arises, blinds get sight.
Here novices come, and until they learn,
Teachers teach, all own will they burn.
Contribution is not counted in any wallet,
Intellectuals appreciate this fortune-fate.

A big building is not the house of knowledge,
It imparts from teacher, book and sage.
Human world is broken, teachers mend,
Picking dispersed flowers, they make garland.
Uneducated pupils are like scattered flowers,
It's a teacher, who picks and puts on towers.

20

Teachers' Day

Laborious and tantalizing sir,
You are a torching teacher,
For each student, you embark,
And fetch light from deep dark.
There are three in the world,
Who hold faith, experience called:
These are Guru, father and mother,
Nothing can be said of other.

A teacher lights inflaming fire,
And fills measureless desire,
Even in a dull student,
To achieve his great achievement.
Guru Jee, without you, what can I do?
With my seven-fold, I bow before you.

21

A Biased Teacher

A teacher motivates his pupils,
To know the world and climb the hills,
A Guru's inspiration works, on level high,
And with consistent struggle, pupils glorify
Their lives' darkness into shining light
So that, in all hazards, they may fight.
Of some counted pupils, he appreciates,
Telling them of their fertile fates.

That way of discrimination, I feel and see,
Fair face with black heart, never inspires me,
unmeasured grief, my soul feels
When the worshipped man kills
Some promising pupils' inspiration...
Then how prosperous will be this nation?

This Cruel Winter

This cruel winter saddened the river,
The edge, the algae and the water shiver.
The white birds, I used to see,
Picking little fishes, where did they flee?
I see around thousand drops of due,
And people are dipping and bathing a few.
In my heart, I feel deeper dent,
O the fishing birds, where you went!

Herds of cattle from grazing yard did come,
To soothe their thirst, and bees did hum
In bushes, then it was the month of summer.
Now the river mourns gazing at less comer.
No hostility, rather it will bear the pain,
For, the river has to meet the winter again.

23

Men's Folly

How beauty lies in the shape of men,
Alas! The pride and vanity made it feign.
A creature, most loved of God,
He poured a soul, making from mud.
Satan played the trick, we paid the cost,
Oh! Eden! A garden of heaven, we lost.
Then He sent on Earth, to be tender as flower,
But forgetting Him, doing sin, we show fleshy-power.

We are mere players, as the couch He sets trace,
Sinking in the sea of sin, we can win no race,
To win, we do sin, knowing heaven's ban,
For transitory pleasures and prolonging pain.
We play in different mood, furious or kind,
But He cares the whole, being sublimed.

24

The Child

On the Earth, a child is much mild,
Created by God, in the world-wild.
It is a sign of innocence, truth and purity,
Mind seems empty, but pregnant with curiosity.
No jealousy, no secret and no hatred,
Mother chuckles, when the baby plays in bed.
Willing to play always in mother's lap,
How the Almighty shaped with pretty shape!

It weeps in hunger, smiles when mother feeds,
She looks, sings, and well wishes, she bids;
Gazing the way of her child's role,
She reminds the Almighty. Oh what a soul!
Innocence, truth and purity, in a child, lie,
when enters the gate of experience, everything die.

25

Human's Duty is Human's Beauty

Human's beauty, has two parts,
One questing self, other is God's arts,
Self questing may shine more well,
If the bestowed beauty goes on God's sail.
Beauty doesn't lie in flesh or fair face,
A body black but heart white, can win the race.
Beauty lies in the duty of men,
And get accordingly, pleasure or pain.

Things are revealed from God to men,
All the secrets are not hidden—
Here fame is not known by ancestor's name,
It is earned by burning in struggle's flame.
In the queue of beauty, all those come,
Who, heartly do handsome.

26

God in a Dream

God, how are you!
To men, what do you do?
How we can look,
The unseen shape you took!
If you are black or white,
When You exist, at day or night!
Are You clothed or naked?
Everything is unique, that You made.

Whom You love, whom You hate,
To whom, come early and to whom late,
When You, mighty power, hold,
When You, weakness, unfold!
How You Saved Your throne!
When Satan, to snatch, was prone.

27

An Ant

It was neither day nor night,
When I saw an inspiring sight;
In drizzling rain and a bit thunder,
An Ant was showing its wonder,
With its tiniest flesh and tiniest legs,
Was carrying its babies, packed in eggs.
To save its babies, it was finding a hole,
And in that Ant, I was finding a soul.

I stood, I gazed and thought of its wisdom,
Oh! Why people talk only of king's kingdom:
A king might have spent life, full of strife,
How peaceful, was this voiceless life!
Lovers and wits can find here charm,
Of living little life in ecstacy, with no harm.

28

Sarcastic Lines

Religious faith is not in dark,
Yet some disloyal-dogs bark;
To make it dark, and bite
The bitches, that desire dogs' might.
Dogs must be aware of—
Who give them feast, are not stuff,
It is bitches' power,
That builds dogs' tower.

The way of barking dogs,
Must not blow fatal fogs,
On bitches' right and ritual,
In the mortal cycle, all are equal.
The venom of power smells
More than the corpses in hells.

29

I

The truth can't lie, I am I,
And I will die too, as I.
I interact with truth and false,
And learn the hidden human's tales.
When the course of time is yours,
To make me tenant, you may force,
But, you can't confine for long,
Soon, I will sing my own song.

Not a destroying dagger or sharp sword,
Can cut 'I', for me, 'I' is a gratifying word.
Keep sympathy away, let me be,what I am,
I'm reluctant to be called by other's name.
I beseech the world. To desert me, do not lie,
I can't be anyone else, so let me die as I.

30

Mighty Tiger

I slouch, I crouch, my eyes flash,
I roar, my mighty chest does clash;
I rule the forest, all around,
When I walk, all fear to utter a sound.
As a hawk, I hunt my prey in you,
My heart has no house for your woo.
By power I am mighty, you are miser,
You live under the paws of a mighty tiger.

From Almighty, I got the ring of king,
Before me, everyone is an inferior being.
Even the singing nightingale goes dumb,
And the saviours of the forest are numb:
Looking my majesty, all the forests fear,
None protests, if someone tries, I tear.

31

The Lung

Toxins are looked by eyes,
And green-wound, by flies.
Saliva drops from the tongue,
You are damaged. O the Lung!
After sipping some sour drops,
You meditate on coveted crops.
You feel grievance at times,
O the Lung! What are your crimes?

You have no foot, move in no way,
Nor can you peep even the Sun's ray.
You are more pious, more mild
Than William Blake's London child,
You are hidden in the ambush of flesh,
Yet, become the prey of a greedy race.

32

How Longer Can I Lie

With panic-heart, and the world blind,
With unseen tears, and depressed mind,
How longer can I lie? 'I'm happy, I'm well,
When the existence reflects in doomed-cell.
Standing on the thorny stake, my life fears,
And waits for the west wind to wipe tears,
Oh! Hopeless, no winds come, no winds care,
I seem solo in a desert, in a world-full-of-fair.

Throngs of people are but the salty water of sea,
That doesn't quench my thirst, nor does solace me.
O Life! How all the hours, you offered plight,
In my full-Moon youth, my black hair got white.
As in forest, I perceive the shadows of wild beast,
Coming near in haste, to make my flesh their feast.

33

The Deceptive One

Wrapped in virgin veil,
Comes and tells a tentative tale.
Unaware of fault or fair,
The Shepherd comes in snare.
In maligned magic, witch is rich,
Words of love, she does preach:
And thus, the river of grief,
Flows under the dried leaf.

The venom of that virgin veil,
Shows the Shepherd, the gate of hell,
Depriving of the virtuous light,
Leaves to play in the path of plight.
But in the toxin of virgin,who cares death,
Until the venom of veil snatches the breath.

34

Life and Death

When life slopes to Dying-Days,
No star, no Moon and no Sun-rays
Stops the sliding down death-prams,
The warmth of life loses its arms.
In a short span of mortality, life hires,
More visions and more desires,
But gripped in the gyre of life and death,
Loses its all, with the loss of breath.

As Iife comes conscious, it bathes in hot blood,
And wants to grow faster as a rainy-river flood.
What existence it has? It holds particles of dust,
And flows with the currents of greed and lust.
Here Life lies on lease, and Death is pretty sure,
When the knots of life break, nothing can cure.

35

Mart of Two Edges

This world is a two-edged mart,
One comes, the other does depart,
Pleasure and pain live side by side,
When pleasure falls, pain does ride.
Let the eyes invade on dense forest,
Falling down of green leaves in haste.
On the naked-trees, Nightingales mourn,
But soon, the green gown of leaves is worn.

Summer has no warmth when winter enters,
The labourers who make palaces, are renters.
When the Sun rises, farmers go on their farm,
Oh! The Moon and stars lose their charm.
Everything rides on two-edged wheel, I mark,
Light is truth, but the worth of light lies in the dark.

36

Unseen Beauty That Came in Dream

Love Sonnets

One night, suddenly it seemed, I did marry,
My sight rested on cheek, that looked like cherry,
And my heart was filled with meta-physical mirth,
Pondering her beauty, on the oblivion Earth.
Then I started to quarrel and to weep,
Before my mom, ''On the shore, is my ship
Of life and learning, in invisible eternity,
My dreams lie, and I was fettered in marriage entity.''

Then my mother consoled me, to sail
My life learning ship, and let her be in veil,
Till I touch the eternity of art,
The bride will bear lonesome, living apart.
Then once again, into her eyes, I looked,
With shyness, she smiled and my heart was hooked.

37

Bud's Beauty

A hidden Bud in tranches,
Beneath the beautiful branches,
Invites the wandering bees to sit,
And to kiss gently, and to fit
His pointed peck-spear
In the branches, and tear
The Bud into full flower,
With melodramatic power.

The Bud germinates to bloom,
Or the garden will go gloom,
The garden demands new corn
To prolong new plant-born.
Then let the Bud bear that pain,
With tickling, to survive the garden.

38

My Goddess

As a heap of dust, I got birth,
And knew nothing, pain or mirth.
Within a year, I lost my father,
Then widow mom, and brother
Decorated my life with flower
And saw me from toe to tower;
Not letting me feel any dearth,
Filled my life with colourful mirth.

As the time passed, the pious heat
Of my spirit, pushed my feet
To visit the Goddess's sphere,
Oh sit! She was found nowhere.
Now, what to say? What to do?
My heart has started to worship you.

39

Inviting Love

Since when, you threw your eye
Into mine,I did not remain I;
My sublimed sense was killed,
And the tender heart was sealed.
Milky cheek and silky hair,
Invite me to have dare
Pointing to strike gently, dear,
Avoiding the sense of fear.

What to say, of slender waist,
It has snatched my ever-rest.
O Love! Where I'm, I'm lost,
The warmth is melting my frost:
So, now my full desire,
Is to burn into your fire.

40

Shyness

With me, this happened first,
I fell in love with no lust,
When I looked her charming beauty,
I prayed, caring for her, must be my duty.
Gradually I became fond,
Of her love and began to love beyond:
Each palpitation of my heart, calls her name,
But shyness! Shyness makes me shame.

Oh! Shyness makes depart everyday,
Thousands of lovers along the Ganges' bay.
What is this shyness? Who will sing?
Shall the same bell, have I to ring?
O Goddess of Love! If my love is unknown,
Then awake her soul and make it known.

41

My Wish

When shall we fly together,
Spreading our own feather—
When shall I chase your charms;
Into my folded arms—
I have earnest appetite of your sweet sound,
And wander as wandering clouds all around,
To make my heart's house in you,
And to make my part, I want to woo.

The beauty of beloved has no worth,
Until her lover gets mirth
Feeling forked feelings,
And having unfathomed willings.
Time is less, darling, come soon,
And let the moment be lovers' boon.

42

Love in Solitude

Since, I was infatuated in love,
I became an elevated Dove:
So, in solitude world, I wish fo fly
Beneath the Sun, above the Moon in the sky,
Where no band of barriers can reach,
We would be the teachers, who love-lesson teach,
On the Moon's bed, in swooning weathers;
Alas! For flying, I have not that feathers.

There my soul would be into yours,
And yours into mine, to feed love-course.
We would colonize there a utopian city,
Where love lives in liberty, and hatred bears pity.
To harm this love, this world turns into a Hurricane,
O Love! Alas! What shall I do, else suffering pain.

43

The Wine of Your Eyes

The bottle of wine lies in your eyes,
Whoever looks into, is intoxicated, alive he dies.
My cup of wine wanders from wine-yard to air,
But to take a drop of wine, it does never dare.
Then, I beseech, let me sip through your lip,
That would intoxicate me deep and deep.
If once, lips with wine are fettered,
The bottle of wine will be scattered;

Then the wine will be turned into sea...
Drowning the gender as she or he.
The life is no life, that lives
Plenty of years, and nothing it perceives.
Then stop me not from sinking in that charms,
If that is poison, let me sip and die in your arms.

44

Hold Your Slippy Tongue

Hold your slippy tongue, and let me give,
My hand into your lonesome hand—
Stop me not, let's play as Adam and Eve,
And let the heaven, once again, be banned.
Everyday the Sun goes and comes again,
This is not the cycle of man, once gone, is gone:
Lone life is pearl, and time, too precise to feign,
Then let's avail the joy of clay, to leave a clone.

Fear not, none has seen the heaven or hell,
Love is God, he brings heaven in lovers' bed;
Hatred is hell, that fetches into a dark dale,
Then let's travel in heaven, in crimson red,
To sow some more new seeds in rapture,
That will prolong after our departure.

45

Floating Love

My Love floats in open sphere
And harvests all the herbs,
That feed Love to keep alive
Providing pleasures to holders.
Mother-Earth is in tense,
Darkness eclipses the Moon,
And the Sun burns in ablaze—
Whose turbulent Love is floating!

She seems in the form of ice,
At the bottom of Pacific Ocean,
Where no rays of the Sun reaches
That may melt the freezing ice;
Yet, my hopeless love floats empty,
From the Lord of Love, gets sympathy.

46

Will Love Come

My fading-faith asks time and again,
Weep not bab! Will your love come?
In my slumber deep,
She comes in dream
And I wish to be lost in that—
But the breaking of night by morning,
Awakes me, and the morning asks,
Awake bab! Is your Love in the bed?

In the evening, I walk on the bank of the Ganga,
And her wave comes to console and sympathize,
But, it hurts too, asking the same—
Stay bab! Have you come alone?
My soul is silent, and faith has died,
Goddess! You should tell, will Love come?

47

You Feared

O love, why you feared,
Without knowing my spirit?
I would never fight
To lit my candle light,
Into your dark house
Breaking into as a brutal-beast.
I would wait, my whole life,
To set my psyche in your psyche.

I would honour your chastity,
Forgetting to quench two thirsty souls.
I'm human, and I have a human heart,
I would preserve that in my attic art.
You damn, die soon, in next birth be bold,
So that you may, my hopeless love, hold.

48

Betrayal in Love

Had you pointed in, to kill
All my sense and desire—
In heart, burning a cruel flame;
Making a lover and then a lame?
O the lady! You did not love,
Giving my heart, a green fuse
You ticked to change my goal,
Never peeping my saddened soul.

My heart is drying up as cut-wood,
No herbs heal, but your love-food:
I know, o the loveless lady, you
Won't come to feed this hungry heart.
Now, on the door of death I lie,
And every moment I live and die.

49

Reminding

To meet, I did wait
Burying the cycle of early or late,
When I changed my faith,
It was the time of my death.
You did not come
To love or to confirm—
Lost in love, I'd no control
Over my disputed soul.

Now I remind, how I was fool,
Losing the sense that was cool
I had started to love more and more,
Now my heart doesn't ache as before.
The bubbling fountain has changed into hiss,
Life is scratched as old walls, now it wants peace.

50

The Untold Moment

Ah! In Black Bee, what the insect
Bites and makes, a sudden erect:
The stream of commotion, he can't hide,
In vein, It begins to flow-faster, inside,
Then the body is gripped in convulsion,
With rhythmic-humming sound, sense is gone,
And he holds the appetite-sufficing organ
Of the flower and sucks, until it goes to damn.

He seems sitting on the supreme tower,
When he unfurls the petals of flower,
Shaking the whole curly crops,
Until the flower is watered with drops.
Beauty vanishes with the fading of petal
So the flower doesn't fight even a bit of battle.

51

Love: Hero of Stage

My soul decorates the stage of love
And invites you to perform—
Bursting your body and dressing your soul
Thrill the visitors in an unconscious world.
All the parts of the body are visitors,
Where Love stands as a hero of the stage.
Without a hero decoration falls apart,
Visitors have no sight, audience, no voice.

I deserve, and assumes an actress of yours,
Love of mine summons yours to accompany:
O sit! You seem a lady of no norms,
Mine is waiting, but yours doesn't come.
Hey heart of stone! Go to a school to be a woman,
And learn the norms of the stage to please the visitors.

52

Love is Divine

The steam of Love, in my heart
Is fueled by the rhythm, of rise and fall,
And divinity, feeds the passion
Of an unseen soul in eternity.
Love is beyond the thought of human,
Which connects human to heaven:
When fragile frame breaks into pieces,
Human remains no human, yet Love remains.

Lovers love, but death deceives...
Their earthly elements may depart
But the invisible being of heavenly Love
Does never depart from lovers' hearts.
When one forgets his body, Love blossoms,
And divinity takes Love to his divine soul.

53

Breaking My Heart

I remember my meta-meeting,
And heart incessantly beating,
For the warm-welcome of new-comer,
But she seemed a dew-drop of summer
That melted with the rising of the heat,
Leaving on the ill-stake of my heart-beat.
As the bud of red roses, she appeared,
The swooning- sound of my heart, she heard.

I started to hover near the bud as a bee
To turn that dew-drop into a passionate sea.
Oh! My heart was hungry of love, she did not feed,
My desires were pricked by thorns, heart began to bleed,
I invoked the fairy of Love,"What hath thou done?
Breaking my heart into pieces, she has gone."

54

Tour to Hill

In love, I was prisoned as poor,
And I willed to have a tour.
I went and ascended the hill,
Met the men of different will,
Gazed rocks, monkeys and hilly trees,
Heart was filled with the touch of breeze.
Suddenly, past memory came in mind,
Eyes were open, sight went blind.

I was on the top of the hill, I remained there,
My happiness fell to bottom to scare
My life, and to eat my meat, bit by bit
From inside, and from head to feet.
Pooh! For her, my love seemed fake,
Now, no tour, with my heart-ache.

55

Lurching Love

Her floppy locks were full of cloud,
That did not darkened love's sphere;
But gave shelter with shade, I was proud,
Her that eyes looked full of intoxication
Which gave me drops in love-cup to drink,
And in the heart, burnt the fire of passion.
She stayed miles away, yet I felt her anklet
Jingling in feet, and I met in dreams by fate.

Now the lurching love falters away,
I feel separation each and every day...
I meet my love with the very passion,
But, her unseen drops have no intoxication.
To knot two threads lie, but it do not tie
Now my psyche thinks, if love does die?

56

Indian Parents

Unrhymed Sonnets

My mom is the *Malkin* of mystery,
And my pop, Pegasus poetry—
For my mortal sense and immortal soul.
I mine the mystery in ecstasy, and take away
Plenty of mystic pearls, yet the mine of mystery is full.
I study Pegasus poetry, it seems so dear
That eclipses Chaucer, Spencer and Shakespeare...
What heaven derives them, they hold unfathomed fame.

Mom's mystery with pious flows, runs in my veins
To keep my blood unspotted and leads to perfection,
In her shadows as queen's treasure, my worthy wings lie
And Pop airs to strengthen, and to fly, high and high:
Her one stroke on my head, excels the bath of seven Ganges,
Wherein, pop's poetry teaches all the philosophy of life.

57

My Niece

When memory goes to grave,
Tears from eyes, drops
And wets all my spiritual crops—
Mind moves in unseen air,
To have a slight sight,
To know, if she is playing in peace.
In a momentary dream
Of my deep slumber;
She seems in her mom's lap,
Parting her lips in smile,
Drinking milk with a little spoon.
When the chirping of cuckoo
Breaks my slumber apart,
Alas! She is no more—

58

The Wheel of Life

The wheel of life is rolling down
And the break is lost in tangles,
Life has become a fearful symmetry
Where alone the fair of graves exists.
It is near the grave, breathing a bit,
Hopping to return back in full-breath,
To be the petals of unaging plant,
And then to blossom for fragrance.

Where is rays of ways of returning back,
When I try, I cry, debris of grief collapses,
I'm grabbed to ground, like a shrunk snake,
In the bitter-winter, and peep from the hole.
I come out, but the debris of grief falls again,
How then I can gather force to lift my head above.

59

Death of a Tree

Those days it was not Ashes—
Glint of Sun rays fell on its leaves
And branches breathed in life,
There would have been roots and trunks,
People would have hoped
Of fruits and flowers—
Those days it would have been
Shelters, and singing theatre
For birds and their youngs,
Many passers-by soothed
Their burning-hearts under its shade,
Singed of scorching sun in the way.
Oh! The foster-mother of many lives!
You died, all went orphans, and death survives.

60

Liberty

If psyche is slave, life lies in sepulcher,
No rays of revolution rise from that...
No burning flames of science, spirit and arts,
Uncounted eyes visit no visions, minds in no reasons,
Fathomed might derives unfathomed might of minds
Like breathless-bodies carrying to graves in coffins.
Slavery affects no end, but prevails here death,
For the fatuous ones, trash is the persisting breath.

Knock mind usurpers away and sparkle the glint of
reasons,
Let the soul master the body, let the psyche sense liberty,
Let the existing breath in earthly-traits be worthy
Sheltering of sparrows under the tree, sitting hawks on top,
Is no eternity but full of fear, woes and pity...
Rage, o the valliant gallants! Supremacy of own mind is
liberty.

61

Fear Me Not

The fluxing time flows faster than the west wind,
And the throngs of people want to fly as herds of birds.
The time flew far, when my head-hair was black,
I lost that in some dale-unfound again,
Measuring as years, months, day and night.
O the thriving world! Come and see, now my hair is white.
We are garlands in the neck of mankind,
Flowers intertwined through the top of thorns,
With a faltering fragrance in brittle bones.
Thousands of buds blushing in branches,
That I had seen blossoming into flowers, faded.
The hues and fragrance with the span of time have gone.
The Soul is heavenly expiated, this body exists for few hours,
Fear me not of vice and virtue, I see mankind in the same flowers.

62

Fire in the Forest

Roaring tiger stroked his tongue to paws
Gasping ''Fire! Fire!'', left to breathe.
Some scattering leaves in the dense forest
were crackling down in ditches,
And the fear of smooth anarchy in birds,
Made them fly high in the sky.
Shadows of unrest spread in the forest,
Little lives on the ground were yearning for life.

The herds of animals were birds,
And the forest ran to vanish under ashes.
Huge trees met their roots with broken waists,
And Nightingales were wailing with fiery-feathers,
In quest of breath, fell in the ditch of death.
Oh! The grace of the green heart became desert.

63

Drops of Rain

Looking some drops of rain,
The land danced in jocund,
For it was after a long drought
And this drought was of harsh summer.
The land that looked green in rainy,
Had been burnt, and become gray,
The grass, trodden by uncounted feet
Was waiting for rain, impatiently.

Now it rains, the grass smiles in green,
And the faded crops laugh in corns.
The land looks it, like a mother
Lookes her happy playing child.
Then the dance of human's crops,
When it rains some more drops.

64

A Featherless Bird

From the pious womb of the mother-bird,
A featherless bird took birth, as a boon
Pleasure overwhelmed in the yard—
Oh! So soon, the little young became doomed,
And saw a corpse in coffin, uff—
The corpse was the mother of the featherless bird...
The little life went orphan, shadows of clouds shed,
And in the peg of pain, its heart was hanged.

When the doomed young grew a little more,
The neighbour birds went whore—
They burnt each grass of the nest
And there were few trees, to give shelter.
It was leaping in woods, picking foods
With full of fear, that hunters may shoot.

Part Three

Short Poems

1

An Author

An author can't be fettered
In the shackles of race,
Religion, nation and his own kinship,
An author is a sparkling glint
For the whole universe.

2

None Wins in War

The history of war is before the eye,
People from here, people from there, die—
Dictators wash their hands in bloody sin,
Applauding win, but in war, none does win.
The song of victory, bathed in blood, we sing,
The beginning of war is the weakness of human being.
O the world! Let the peace blossom on the Earth,
To save the present, and the coming birth.

3

Love and Like

Love and like aren't alike,
Love cherishes—
And lives in the Palace of infinity:
Love is the son of Metaphysical-Mother,
Where Like lives in the cottage of anatomy,
It perishes in an un-said time,
Like is the son of Somatic-Mother.

4

The Rich Soul

I may be poor of worldly wealth,
But in richness, my soul floats,
Empty innate kicks, the outer wealth,
And gets the feast from Godly pots.

God does oft teach—
With unseen ink in his pen,
''None is poor, none is rich,
Nothing is yours, that you gain;
So, not to tumble in illusion's gyre,
I am ice, I am fire.''

5

A Little Insect

Trough water or earth,
Tiny life comes in birth,
And in curved lease, warns the wisest,
Pride snatches the ever rest,
And in the mode of straight,
Leads to God, to fix its faith.

6

The Sky

When I look up the sky,
My extreme will arouses high,
To fly in the open sphere,
Collecting love and killing my fear.

Glimpsing stars eclipse my pain,
Breaking apart my slavery chain:
And wage the way to eternal bliss,
To calm the soul and get peace.

7

O Love

Oh! Love!
You have no hand,
To write love—

        Then?
       Hold the pen,
With your foot-fingers-tip,
And write on my dried lip,
As nectar, my lip will sip,
And in the heart, it will go deep.

8

Where is Demon

A Demon was there, my leg-behind,
And a pair of eyes, was peeping—
In awe of life, fear for safe soul,
I cleansed my heart, then held His Arts,
The eternity of the soul broke the fear in parts.

Then my heart questioned
In unheard voice, yet He heard,
And replied, "Where is Demon,
The evil deeds of very human,
Gives the birth of Demon".

9

Now Summer Begins

Now the swooning summer begins,
The west wind is amazed at—
How Autumn unveiled the veil,
In hope of enjoying Summer naked.
Autumn loves the forest leafless...
With the panic-cry of Nightingales.
Now the passionate Summer is waiting,
To sweat the pairs in double drops.

10

The Heap of Flesh

My body is a heap of flesh,
Since, one day it will mingle in dust,
For wealth, let me not have lust,
But, let me learn the ways,
In which, I may live my present days.

11

A Lock

A small lock, locks a big room,
And a key, smaller than the lock,
Unlocks the locked room.
When an ant enters—
Into the hoof of an elephant,
The pride of being vast,
Collapses on the surface.
A leafless body that is man,
Has pride, is he wise or insane?

12

A Mosquito

A mosquito sits on man,
And sucks the blood,
The man feels much pain,
Sometimes kills the mosquito—

A man lives on the Earth,
Mines much from her womb,
And the Earth is being hollowed,
And she says nothing...

13

Midnight on Phone

When the Day goes in the arms of Darkness,
At midnight, eyes quest some face,
When get, gossip begins with—
How are you? What do you do?
Then slowly changes the rhythm,
With melodramatic, as honey bees hum.
The fragile- frame stays as stable,
But what to call the loosening sense...
It loses, then burns in unseen fire
And both the sides, it burns within,
Till the dew drops of dawn.

14

My Thoughts

What human light can peep into—
Another's inner sight?
I do not know if He exists or not,
But, if He exists, then He can peep
Everyone's inner sight, deep.

People are moulded into touched circumstance,
Hair turns white, yet learning has no perfection.
The wisdom of a bird is always like a bud,
Before the wisdom blossoms in full flower,
O, the unseen King! The bird mingles in mud.

15

Unseen Worm

Some unseen burning worm, not in fire,
But in some unseen fuel,
Provokes two living-leaves—
The two leaves do not turn into ashes;
But get the bottom of Pacific Ocean,
After losing some worms in existence.
This unseen worm comes again...
On the surface, and sets the fire to burn,
The burning of the fire without woods
Retains the way of procreation on the Earth.

16

Pain

Pain is but, purifier,
Purifier of the soul and mind,
It washes all the ill-thoughts away—
That germinates in mind, but...
Assumes the soul to be a counterpart.
Innocent soul, overwhelmed of physical world,
Fights alone, and is wounded—
By the collisions of physical walls.

Then the stream of pain flows,
Through the eternal veins—
To wash the odorous smell of bad-blood,
And to purify the soul.

17

Two Incidents of Life

When I ponder, I find,
Two incidents of life—
One has happened,
That was inserting of breath;
The other is rest,
That is death.

18

Softy

We ate softy there,
The taste was very delicious,
And more delicious was—
The gossips, we guys did there,
That day—
Natural grin on faces,
We witnessed one another.
It was those days—
When the burdens of ours,
Were on our parents' shoulders...

Long after, I passed alone,
Through the very softy-shop,
I stood, I ate—
People witnessed my face,
Full of frustration and tense,
For, the burdens were—
On my own shoulder.

19

Conspiracy

The conch was shrunk,
Placed on a tree trunk,
With whistling sound,
Here, there, all-around.

Passed unaware, the knell,
Singing of heaven and hell,
Today the tiger did not tear...
Yet, it was the doomed deer.

It was every cruel-creature,
That thrashed innocence, with its fur,
With conspiring couch, that did conspire,
And the innocent deer came into the gyre.

20

Bud in the Creepers

It came in thin branches,
With lighting-lips in smile,
And unaware of its hues—
Like autumn's dappled dews.

It threw its armor away,
And came out like a warrior of beauty,
With fragrance, it blossomed—
A bee was in queue, soon he hummed.

It was lulled by that bee—
With applauding words, and tantalizing tones,
In deep slumber, the passionate flower slept,
And then with no hues and fragrance, it was left.

21

My Treasure

She loved me,
I did not—
She loved me unfathomed,
Yet I did not—
All her kinships, she left behind,
She began to find her happiness in me,
She assumed me her jewelry and life-treasure;
Yet my heart did not melt in her love-cup—
She unlocked the engraved box of her life,
From her birth to her adultery,
And yet, I loved her not—
She pledged, not to live
Without her life-treasure,
She urged,"She is in the sea
Of nothingness with pricking-pain,
Without her life-treasure."
Yet, I loved her not—

But, I love—
I love the ways, she loves,

I love her determination in love,
I love her adamant faith in love—
Oh! In fact she is my treasure,
She is the treasure of love and spirituality,
Gifted me by Almighty,
Hence, I do not want to lose her ever.

22

Two Drops of Rain

Like magnet, it draws inwards,
Within minutes, it travels to top,
Of the imagined mountain...
On the mountain top,
The shadows of summer prevails,
Here two pinch of soil,
Holds the happiness of the world,
Souls in soil play in ecstacy—
Consuming fragile-frame.

Then two drops of rain—
Ah! collapses the mountain.

23

Morning Says Something

Marvelous Morning's miracle,
Says to sleeping soul, some secret,
To take-off tattered thought
And accept arising aught.

Morning makes men mind,
Of opening opinion of oblation,
Forgetting flattery and fellow-fight,
Letting the lamp light lineal lights.

Nasty notions nurture nothing,
So sail in super sanitation.
Bargain bright, be bold,
Gamble good, gain good.

24

The Sun and the Moon

The Sun comes, the Moon goes,
The Moon comes, the Sun goes,
He gives energy and daylight,
She gives pleasure, shining at night.

One comes in rose, other in jasmine,
Both have charming and lovely scene;
Mothers tell, wo! Look at! What a sight!
All crying children go silent and see the sight.

25

Twin Brothers

You are well, I am good,
Mom gives us early food,
You awake, I arise,
You are brave, I am wise.

You write and I read,
We are of the same seed,
Father brings toys for us,
We become happy thus.

26

Life in Trap

I was trapped in a cold meed and mire
Suffering from shivering, and desiring fire.
I was kicking with full force to get rid,
From inside drowning mire, pricking thorns and meed.

Dire was the tiger, I was the deer,
The deer was in tiger's jaw, filled with fear,
No neighbour came to help me—
I was crying, and in my heart, a fearful sea.

The dire was vast, and difficult to extricate,
The sun of my life was setting, so I rebuked my fate,
Fluttered my wings as a victim-bird in the peck of parasite,
And kicked the dire down, to keep my life in light.

About the Author

About the Author's Life

Ranjan Yadav was born on April 30, 1991, in a village, named Asnatari, PO- Tonapathar, PS- Suiya, Panchayat- Dhanuwasar, District- Banka, State- Bihar (India). His father Lakho Yadav, was a poor farmer who had a small clay-house and less field to farm crops, so he used to go to other state to work as a laborer to bring up his family. Once his father sowed some crops in the field and went to Kolkata to earn some money, but alas! He did never return back, he died there, his mother Ramsakhia Devi wanted to see the dead-body of his father but there was none to bring his dead body home, hence she could not see the corpse of his father.

As an unfortunate child, The poet lost his father only at the age of six months. He could not save in his mind, even the picture of his father. He has four brothers as: Narayan, Gopal, Bachchu and the poet himself as the youngest brother in all, and one sister, Manju.

After the death of his father, it was very difficult for his mother, Ramsakhia Devi, to bring up five children.

There was not any source of income for her, suddenly she came in such a thorny and difficult world, from where no path looked to go. She cried and mourned in darkness for days, but she had to step forward for the sake of her five children, so she gathered courage looking at the faded-faces of her children. She started to work hard, she gathered day and night in a single bowl for the sake of her children. Anyhow she wanted to keep her children happy, so she used to go to Biharo forest, five kilometers far from home, to pluck *Beedi*-leaves and in the evening she went to another village to sell the *Beedi*-leaves. After some years, the poet's maternal-grandmother gave a buffalo to his mother and it was a tiny source of income now. She grazed, cut green-grass, milked the buffalo herself and went on foot to Suiya market to sell milk.

Narayan, the poet's eldest brother lived at maternal-house, Barguniya. He had a deep desire for study, so he used to study there, but after the death of his father he left his study and went to Kolkata to work as a laborer, only at the age of twelve years because he wanted to support his mother. After two or three years, the second eldest brother, Gopal also went to the same city to earn money and support his mother. Hence no sibling could attain even the basic education except the poet.

The Author's Education

Getting education in such a village, where there is no school, no road and no teacher to teach, was crossing a deep sea without a ship. Though no member from the family of the poet was educated and even after the death of his father, his mother Ramsakhia Devi and all his elder brothers wanted him to study. But how can one study without school and teacher? There was no school to go, and no teacher to teach, nor the family was in good economic-condition that the poet could be sent out of the village to study, staying there.

But the poet was a bud filled with aroma in the house of mud. He too wanted to study since his very childhood but due to not having any teacher in the village, he was not able to start his study. Then his second elder brother, Gopal, went to another village to find a teacher to teach as tuition. Gopal met a young man, named Jitendra Kumar in Tari village and told him to teach coming at home. Thanks to the young man, he accepted this proposal and he used to come for one hour to teach the poet and the education of the poet started thus.

Then the poet got his admission in a State gov. primary school. It is three kilometers far from his own village. In the way there are river and mountain, no clear path to go to the school, and the path was full of sharp pointed-pebbles and stones, where the poet used to go with naked sole, he had no slippers to wear, and no friend to go with. Sometimes he feared ghosts while passing in the way alone, yet he did miss his class rarely. Then he got his admission in a middle school at Suiya, that is five kilometers far from his village and he alone used to go and come on foot. Whenever there was heavy work at home, the poet did not go to school on the advice of his mother, he went to graze buffaloes and goats in nearby fields and hills. He used to carry books, copies and pens with him while grazing buffaloes and goats. Problems were playing with his fate, but the poet as an optimistic warrior kept on fighting for his study.In 2009, he passed his matriculation anyhow, from High School Suiya Ghuthiya and decided to leave his home for his further education. In 2009, he got his admission in S.S.P.Y. College Katoria Banka in intermediate class, and from 2009 to 2011 he stayed at the hostel provided by the college.

In 2011, he was registered in Tilka Manjhi Bhagalpur University Bhagalpur as a student of Bachelor of Arts in English Literature. Hence he left Katoria and went to Bhagalpur. As he came from a quite unprivileged village, English seemed as the most difficult subject for him, so he took it as a challenge and laboured very hard. He became a voracious reader of English Literature and grammar. He studied day and night to have a strong hold in English and joined some coachings to learn to communicate in English. With the passage of time he became a very good speaker and he learnt American as well as British accent in English communication. In 2015, he passed his Bachelor of Arts and became the first man to have a Bachelor Degree in his village.

In 2015, he got his admission in PG Department of English as a student of Post Graduate in English Literature. In the Department, he was a very good student. All the students of the Department called him, ''Ranjan Jee''. He completed his Post Graduate in 2018. From 2019 to 2021 he was engaged in the course of Bachelor of Education (B.Ed.)

In 2021 he married to Sinni Rani. She is a well educated girl. She is a Master of Science in Mathematics and Bachelor of Education (B.Ed.) from TMBU Bhagalpur. When she knew that her husband is a writer, she encouraged and inspired him to write more and more and to get them publish. She is very helpful, careful and supportive.

Being inspired from the condition of his childhood and from his family, the poet has decided to get more and more higher education. And now in 2022, he is pursuing his PhD Degree from TMBU Bhagalpur. He has been teaching as a tuition teacher since his Bachelor Degree to support his study. Though his mother and brothers supported him, yet sometimes he felt the scarcity of money, so he taught for the sake of money, but gradually teaching became his hobby and now he teaches students enthusiastically.

The poet (Ranjan Yadav)